Learn all about Spring Boot: Building Modern Java Applications

"Learn Spring Boot (Java): Building Modern Java Applications" serves as a comprehensive guide for individuals interested in developing Java applications using the Spring Boot framework. Through twelve chapters covering a wide range of topics, readers will gain a strong foundation in Spring Boot development, including web application development, database integration, RESTful services, authentication and authorization, testing, microservices, deployment, and advanced topics. By exploring these topics and applying the provided examples and techniques, readers will be empowered to build robust and scalable Java applications using Spring Boot.

The book covers the following:

Chapter 1: Introduction to Spring Boot

Overview of Spring Boot and its advantages in Java application development.

Setting up the development environment for Spring Boot.

Understanding the Spring Boot architecture and key components.

Creating and running your first Spring Boot application.

Exploring Spring Boot documentation and resources.

Chapter 2: Getting Started with Spring Boot

Introduction to the Spring Framework and its core concepts.

Building RESTful APIs with Spring Boot.

Creating controllers and mapping requests to endpoints.

Utilizing Spring Boot's dependency management and auto-configuration features.

Testing and debugging Spring Boot applications.

Chapter 3: Building Web Applications with Spring Boot

Working with web views and templates in Spring Boot.

Utilizing Spring Boot's MVC (Model-View-Controller) framework.

Handling form submissions and data validation in Spring Boot.

Securing web applications with Spring Security.

Integrating front-end frameworks with Spring Boot, such as Angular or React.

Chapter 4: Database Integration with Spring Boot

Working with relational databases in Spring Boot.

Configuring and connecting to databases using Spring Data.

Performing CRUD (Create, Read, Update, Delete) operations with Spring Boot.

Implementing data validation and constraints.

Utilizing Spring Data JPA for object-relational mapping.

Chapter 5: Building RESTful Services with Spring Boot

Implementing RESTful APIs using Spring Boot.

Handling HTTP methods and request/response payloads.

Implementing authentication and authorization with Spring Security.

Utilizing Spring Boot's support for HATEOAS (Hypermedia as the Engine of Application State).

Versioning and documenting RESTful APIs with Spring Boot.

Chapter 6: Data Validation and Error Handling

Validating request data using Spring Boot's validation framework.

Handling and customizing validation errors in Spring Boot.

Implementing global exception handling and error responses.

Utilizing custom exception handlers and error handling strategies.

Logging and monitoring errors in Spring Boot applications.

Chapter 7: Caching and Performance Optimization

Utilizing Spring Boot's caching mechanisms for improved performance.

Configuring caching providers, such as Redis or Ehcache.

Caching strategies and best practices for different use cases.

Implementing performance optimizations, such as lazy loading and caching of expensive operations.

Monitoring and analyzing application performance using Spring Boot Actuator.

Chapter 8: Authentication and Authorization

Implementing user authentication and authorization using Spring Security.

Configuring authentication providers, such as databases or LDAP.

Role-based and permission-based access control in Spring Boot.

Implementing OAuth 2.0 for secure API authentication and authorization.

Utilizing JSON Web Tokens (JWT) for stateless authentication.

Chapter 9: Testing Spring Boot Applications

Introduction to testing methodologies in Spring Boot.

Writing unit tests and integration tests for Spring Boot applications.

Utilizing testing frameworks, such as JUnit and Mockito.

Testing Spring MVC controllers and RESTful APIs.

Testing database interactions and using test doubles.

Chapter 10: Building Microservices with Spring Boot

Introduction to microservices architecture and its benefits.

Designing and implementing microservices using Spring Boot.

Service discovery and communication between microservices.

Implementing fault tolerance and resilience in microservices.

Deploying and scaling microservices with Spring Cloud.

Chapter 11: Deployment and DevOps with Spring Boot

Packaging and deploying Spring Boot applications.

Configuring production-ready features with Spring Boot Actuator.

Utilizing containerization technologies, such as Docker, for Spring Boot applications.

Continuous integration and deployment (CI/CD) with Spring Boot.

Monitoring and logging Spring Boot applications in production.

Chapter 12: Best Practices and Advanced Topics

Implementing security best practices in Spring Boot applications.

Optimizing Spring Boot applications for scalability and performance.

Design patterns and architectural considerations for Spring Boot applications.

Utilizing Spring Boot's support for messaging and event-driven architectures.

Exploring advanced topics, such as Spring Batch for batch processing or Spring WebFlux for reactive programming.

Chapter 1: Introduction to Spring Boot

Spring Boot is a Java-based framework used for creating microservices. It is a part of the Spring Framework and is used to simplify the creation of stand-alone, production-grade Spring-based applications.

Spring Boot is a opinionated framework that makes it easy to create stand-alone, production-grade Spring-based Applications. It favors convention over configuration and is used to simplify the creation of stand-alone, production-grade Spring-based applications.

Spring Boot is a great way to get started with Spring. It provides a wide variety of features that can be used to create stand-alone, production-grade Spring-based applications.

Some of the features that Spring Boot provides are:

- Automatic configuration: Spring Boot can automatically configure your application based on the dependencies you have added. For example, if you add the H2 database dependency, Spring Boot will automatically configure an in-memory database.

- Embedded servers: Spring Boot can provide an embedded Tomcat or Jetty server to run your application. This is useful when you want to deploy your application as a war file.

- Command line interface: Spring Boot provides a CLI that can be used to create, run and test Spring-based applications.

- Actuator: Spring Boot provides an Actuator that can be used to monitor and manage your application.

Overview of Spring Boot and its advantages in Java application development.

Spring Boot is a Java-based framework that provides a simplified, convention-based approach to developing Spring applications. It is designed to reduce the amount of boilerplate code and configuration that is required to build Spring-based applications.

Spring Boot provides a number of advantages over traditional Spring-based application development:

1. It reduces the amount of boilerplate code and configuration required.

2. It favors convention over configuration, making it easier to get started with.

3. It provides built-in support for a number of common development tasks, such as logging, caching, and monitoring.

4. It makes it easy to create and run stand-alone Spring-based applications.

5. It provides production-ready features, such as metrics and health checks, out of the box.

Setting up the development environment for Spring Boot.

There are a few different ways that you can set up the development environment for Spring Boot. One way is to use the Spring Boot CLI, which is a command line tool that can be used to create and run Spring Boot applications. Another way is to use the Spring Boot Initializr, which is a web-based tool that can be used to create and generate Spring Boot projects. Finally, you can also use the Spring Tool Suite, which is an Eclipse-based IDE that comes with everything you need to develop Spring Boot applications.

Understanding the Spring Boot architecture and key components.

Spring Boot is a Java-based framework used for creating microservices. It is a lightweight framework that comes with a lot of features to reduce the boilerplate code.

Some of the key components of Spring Boot are:

- **Auto-configuration:** This is one of the key features of Spring Boot. It automatically configures the application based on the dependencies present in the classpath.
- **Embedded servers:** Spring Boot comes with embedded servers which makes it easy to deploy and test the applications.
- **Starter dependencies:** Spring Boot provides starter dependencies to get the required dependencies for a particular type of application. For example, if we

want to create a web application, we can include the spring-boot-starter-web dependency in our pom.xml file.

- **Actuator:** Spring Boot Actuator is used to monitor and manage the application. It provides a lot of endpoints to get information about the application.

Creating and running your first Spring Boot application.

Spring Boot is a framework that allows you to easily create stand-alone, production-grade Spring-based Applications. It takes an opinionated view of the Spring platform and third-party libraries so you can get started with minimum fuss. Most Spring Boot applications need very little Spring configuration.

Creating a Spring Boot application is easy using the Spring Initializr. The Initializr provides a fast way to create a Spring Boot project. It will generate a Maven build file and a Spring Boot application with the required dependencies.

To create a Spring Boot application, you need to first create a Maven build file. You can do this using the Spring Initializr. The Initializr provides a fast way to create a Spring Boot project. It will generate a Maven build file and a Spring Boot application with the required dependencies.

Once you have created the Maven build file, you can then run the application using the Spring Boot Maven plugin. This plugin will start the application on an embedded Tomcat server.

To run the application, you can use the following command:

```
mvn spring-boot:run
```

This will start the application on an embedded Tomcat server.

Exploring Spring Boot documentation and resources.

Spring Boot is a popular framework for developing Java applications. It is designed to make it easy to create stand-alone, production-grade Spring-based applications.

The Spring Boot documentation is a great resource for learning about the framework. It includes tutorials, guides, and reference material. The documentation is well organized and easy to navigate.

There are also a number of other resources available for learning about Spring Boot. These include blog posts, video tutorials, and online courses. Spring Boot is a very popular framework, so there is a wealth of information available.

If you are just getting started with Spring Boot, it is recommended that you start with the documentation. Once you have a basic understanding of the framework, you can then explore the other resources available.

Chapter 2: Getting Started with Spring Boot

Introduction to the Spring Framework and its core concepts.

Spring is a popular Java application framework and Spring Boot is an extension of that which makes it easy to create stand-alone, production-grade Spring-based applications.

Spring Boot is designed to get you up and running as quickly as possible, with minimal configuration. It takes an opinionated view of the Spring platform, and gets you up and running with the minimum amount of fuss.

At its core, Spring Boot is just Spring, so if you know how to use the Spring framework, you're already halfway there!

The key features of Spring Boot are:

Automatic configuration - Spring Boot automatically configures your application based on the dependencies you have on your classpath. For example, if you add the H2 database driver to your classpath, Spring Boot will automatically configure an in-memory database for you.

Standalone - Spring Boot applications can be run as standalone Java applications or deployed to a servlet container. There is no need to deploy a WAR file to an application server.

Embedded servers - Spring Boot comes with a number of embedded servers, including Tomcat, Jetty and Undertow. This means you can run your application as a standalone Java application with no need to deploy it to an application server.

Metrics - Spring Boot provides built-in support for a number of metrics, including CPU, memory, and disk usage.

Health checks - Spring Boot provides a number of built-in health checks, which can be used to monitor the health of your application.

Externalized configuration - Spring Boot allows you to externalize your configuration, so that you can easily switch between different environments (e.g. development, test, and production).

Application monitoring - Spring Boot provides a number of tools to help you monitor your application, including a web interface, JMX beans, and a command-line tool.

Spring Boot is a great way to get up and running quickly with the Spring framework. It takes care of a lot of the boilerplate configuration and allows you to focus on your application's functionality.

Building RESTful APIs with Spring Boot.

RESTful APIs are built on the Representational State Transfer (REST) architectural style. Spring Boot is a Java-based framework that makes it easy to create stand-alone, production-grade Spring-based Applications that you can "just run".

In this chapter, we'll cover the following topics:

An introduction to the REST architectural style

Creating a simple RESTful API with Spring Boot

Configuring Spring Boot for MySQL

Testing our API with Postman

What is REST?

REST is an architectural style for building web services. It is based on the principles of statelessness, client-server communication, layering, and code on demand.

RESTful web services are built on the HTTP protocol, and use the HTTP methods (GET, POST, PUT, DELETE) to specify the operations that they support.

RESTful web services are typically organized around resources, which are the units of information that they expose. A resource is typically a noun, such as "user" or "product".

Creating a Simple REST API

We're going to use Spring Boot to build our API. Spring Boot is a Java-based framework that makes it easy to create stand-alone, production-grade Spring-based Applications that you can "just run".

We're going to use the following tools to build our API:

Spring Boot

MySQL

Maven

Postman

First, we'll create a Maven project in Eclipse.

In the New Project dialog, select Maven > Maven Project.

Click Next.

In the New Maven Project dialog, select the Create a simple project checkbox.

Click Next.

In the New Maven Project dialog, enter the following information:

Group Id: com.example

Artifact Id: spring-boot-rest-api

Version: 0.0.1-SNAPSHOT

Packaging: jar

Click Finish.

Eclipse will create a Maven project with the following structure:

Next, we'll add the following dependencies to our pom.xml file:

spring-boot-starter-data-jpa

mysql-connector-java

spring-boot-starter-web

The spring-boot-starter-data-jpa dependency will add the Spring Data JPA library to our project. The Spring Data JPA library makes it easy to work with JPA in a Spring-based application.

The mysql-connector-java dependency will add the MySQL JDBC driver to our project. This will allow us to connect to a MySQL database from our Java code.

The spring-boot-starter-web dependency will add the Spring MVC and Tomcat libraries to our project. This will allow us to build a web application that can handle HTTP requests and responses.

Our pom.xml file should now look like this:

```xml
<?xml version="1.0" encoding="UTF-8"?> <project
xmlns="http://maven.apache.org/POM/4.0.0"
xmlns:xsi="http://www.w3.org/2001/XMLSchem
a-instance"
xsi:schemaLocation="http://maven.apache.org/P
OM/4.0.0 http://maven.apache.org/xsd/maven-
4.0.0.xsd"> <modelVersion>4.0.0</modelVersion>
<groupId>com.example</groupId>
<artifactId>spring-boot-rest-api</artifactId>
<version>0.0.1-SNAPSHOT</version>
<packaging>jar</packaging> <name>spring-boot-
rest-api</name> <description>Demo project for
Spring Boot</description> <parent>
<groupId>org.springframework.boot</groupId>
<artifactId>spring-boot-starter-
parent</artifactId>
<version>2.0.3.RELEASE</version>
<relativePath/> <!-- lookup parent from
repository --> </parent> <properties>
<project.build.sourceEncoding>UTF-
8</project.build.sourceEncoding>
<project.reporting.outputEncoding>UTF-
8</project.reporting.outputEncoding>
<java.version>1.8</java.version> </properties>
<dependencies> <dependency>
<groupId>org.springframework.boot</groupId>
<artifactId>spring-boot-starter-data-
jpa</artifactId> </dependency> <dependency>
<groupId>mysql</groupId> <artifactId>mysql-
connector-java</artifactId>
```

```xml
<scope>runtime</scope> </dependency>
<dependency>
<groupId>org.springframework.boot</groupId>
<artifactId>spring-boot-starter-web</artifactId>
</dependency> <dependency>
<groupId>org.springframework.boot</groupId>
<artifactId>spring-boot-starter-test</artifactId>
<scope>test</scope> </dependency>
</dependencies> <build> <plugins> <plugin>
<groupId>org.springframework.boot</groupId>
<artifactId>spring-boot-maven-
plugin</artifactId> </plugin> </plugins>
</build> </project>
```

Next, we'll create a Spring Boot application class. This class will configure our application and bootstrap it.

Create a new Java class in the com.example.springbootrestapi package, and name it Application.java.

Add the following annotations to the Application class:

@SpringBootApplication

@EnableJpaRepositories

The @SpringBootApplication annotation is used to configure and bootstrap a Spring Boot application.

The @EnableJpaRepositories annotation is used to enable Spring Data JPA in our application.

Our Application class should now look like this:

```
package com.example.springbootrestapi; import
org.springframework.boot.SpringApplication;
import
org.springframework.boot.autoconfigure.SpringBo
otApplication; import
org.springframework.data.jpa.repository.config.En
ableJpaRepositories; @SpringBootApplication
@EnableJpaRepositories public class Application {
public static void main(String[] args) {
SpringApplication.run(Application.class, args); } }
```

Next, we'll create a Spring Data JPA repository for our User entity.

Create a new Java interface in the com.example.springbootrestapi.repository package, and name it UserRepository.

Add the following annotations to the UserRepository interface:

@Repository

@Transactional

The @Repository annotation is used to mark a class as a Spring Data JPA repository.

The @Transactional annotation is used to mark a method as being transactional.

Our UserRepository interface should now look like this:

```
package
com.example.springbootrestapi.repository; import
org.springframework.data.jpa.repository.JpaRepos
itory; import
org.springframework.data.jpa.repository.Query;
import
org.springframework.data.repository.query.Param
; import
org.springframework.stereotype.Repository;
import
org.springframework.transaction.annotation.Trans
```

actional; import
com.example.springbootrestapi.model.User;
@Repository @Transactional public interface
UserRepository extends JpaRepository<User,
Long> { @Query("SELECT u FROM User u WHERE
u.email = :email") User
findByEmail(@Param("email") String email); }

Next, we'll create a Spring Data JPA entity for our
User.

Create a new Java class in the
com.example.springbootrestapi.model package,
and name it User.

Add the following annotations to the User class:

@Entity

@Table

The @Entity annotation is used to mark a class as
a JPA entity.

The @Table annotation is used to specify the name
of the database table that this entity will be
mapped to.

Our User class should now look like this:

package com.example.springbootrestapi.model;
import javax.persistence.Column; import
javax.persistence.Entity; import
javax.persistence.GeneratedValue; import
javax.persistence.GenerationType; import
javax.persistence.Id; import
javax.persistence.Table; @Entity @Table(name =
"users") public class User { @Id
@GeneratedValue(strategy =
GenerationType.IDENTITY) private Long id;
@Column(name = "first_name") private String
firstName; @Column(name = "last_name") private
String lastName; private String email; // Getters
and setters omitted for brevity }

Next, we'll create a Spring MVC controller for our
API.

Create a new Java class in the com.example

Creating controllers and mapping requests to endpoints with Spring Boot.

In Spring Boot, controllers are responsible for handling incoming HTTP requests and mapping them to the appropriate endpoint. Endpoints are the URLs that clients can use to access your application.

To create a controller, you first need to create a class that annotated with @Controller . For example:

```
@Controller public class MyController { // ... }
```

Once you have created a controller, you can map requests to endpoints by using the @RequestMapping annotation. For example:

```
@RequestMapping("/endpoint") public String handleRequest() { // ... }
```

The @RequestMapping annotation can be used to specify the HTTP method that a particular endpoint should be mapped to. For example, if you want to map an endpoint to the GET method, you would use the @GetMapping annotation.

```
@GetMapping("/endpoint") public String
handleRequest() { // ... }
```

If you want to map an endpoint to the POST method, you would use the @PostMapping annotation.

```
@PostMapping("/endpoint") public String
handleRequest() { // ... }
```

You can also map an endpoint to multiple HTTP methods by using the @RequestMapping annotation with the methods attribute. For example:

```
@RequestMapping(value = "/endpoint", method =
{ RequestMethod.GET, RequestMethod.POST })
public String handleRequest() { // ... }
```

Utilizing Spring Boot's dependency management and auto-configuration features.

Spring Boot's dependency management and auto-configuration features are two of its most powerful tools. By managing dependencies, Spring Boot is able to provide a consistent and easy-to-use experience across a wide variety of applications. And by auto-configuring your application, Spring Boot can provide a significant amount of boilerplate configuration that would otherwise be required.

Dependency management is a crucial part of any application, and Spring Boot makes it easy to manage dependencies with its built-in dependency management system. Spring Boot automatically resolves dependencies for your application, and provides a consistent experience across different applications.

Auto-configuration is another powerful feature of Spring Boot. By auto-configuring your application, Spring Boot can provide a significant amount of boilerplate configuration that would otherwise be required. This can save you a lot of time and effort, and can make your application more consistent and easier to use.

Testing and debugging Spring Boot applications.

Testing and debugging Spring Boot applications can be done using a number of different tools and techniques. In this section, we will discuss some of the most commonly used tools and techniques for testing and debugging Spring Boot applications.

One of the most important tools for testing and debugging Spring Boot applications is the Spring Boot Developer Tools. The Spring Boot Developer Tools are a set of tools that allow developers to quickly and easily test and debug Spring Boot applications. The Spring Boot Developer Tools include a number of features, such as the ability to automatically restart applications when changes are made, and the ability to debug applications using a remote debugger.

Another tool that can be used for testing and debugging Spring Boot applications is the Spring Boot Test Suite. The Spring Boot Test Suite is a set of tools that allow developers to quickly and easily create and run unit tests for Spring Boot applications. The Spring Boot Test Suite includes a number of features, such as the ability to automatically run tests when changes are made to the code, and the ability to generate code coverage reports.

Finally, the Spring Boot Actuator is a tool that can be used for monitoring and managing Spring Boot applications. The Spring Boot Actuator includes a number of features, such as the ability to view application logs, and the ability to view application metrics.

Chapter 3: Building Web Applications with Spring Boot

Working with web views and templates in Spring Boot.

Web views and templates are a common way to build web applications with Spring Boot. There are many ways to work with web views and templates in Spring Boot, but the most common way is to use the Thymeleaf template engine. Thymeleaf is a popular template engine that allows you to easily create and render HTML pages. It also has excellent support for working with CSS and JavaScript. In this chapter, we will cover how to use Thymeleaf to create and render web pages in Spring Boot.

Utilizing Spring Boot's MVC (Model-View-Controller) framework.

The MVC (Model-View-Controller) framework is a popular design pattern for web applications. Spring Boot is a framework that makes it easy to create web applications using the MVC pattern. In

this chapter, we'll look at how to use Spring Boot
to create a web application that uses the MVC
pattern. We'll start by creating a simple web page
that displays a message. Then we'll add a
controller that handles requests from the web
page. Finally, we'll add a model that stores data for
the web page.

Handling form submissions and data validation in Spring Boot.

Form submissions and data validation is a critical
part of any web application. Spring Boot makes it
easy to handle form submissions and data
validation by providing built-in support for both.

When a form is submitted, Spring Boot
automatically binds the form data to a JavaBean.
This makes it easy to process the form data in your
controller. Spring Boot also provides built-in
support for data validation. This makes it easy to
validate form data before it is processed by your
controller.

To handle form submissions, you need to add a
@Controller annotation to your controller class.
This enables Spring Boot to automatically map
form submissions to your controller methods.

To validate form data, you need to add a @Valid annotation to your controller method. This tells Spring Boot to validate the form data before it is processed by your controller method.

You can also add a @Validated annotation to your controller method. This tells Spring Boot to validate the form data and to automatically return a 400 Bad Request status code if the data is not valid.

You can use the @InitBinder annotation to customize how Spring Boot binds form data to JavaBeans. This is useful if you need to convert the data in the form to a different data type or format.

You can use the @ModelAttribute annotation to access form data that is not bound to a JavaBean. This is useful if you need to access form data that is not part of your model.

Spring Boot makes it easy to handle form submissions and data validation. By using the built-in support for both, you can easily build web applications that are both user-friendly and reliable.

Securing web applications with Spring Security.

Spring Security is a framework that provides authentication, authorization, and protection against common web attacks. It is the de-facto standard for securing Spring-based applications.

Spring Security is a powerful and highly customizable authentication and access-control framework. It enables developers to build secure web applications by providing a comprehensive set of security features.

Spring Security offers a comprehensive set of features for securing web applications. These features can be divided into the following categories:

Authentication: Spring Security provides a wide range of authentication mechanisms, including form-based authentication, HTTP basic authentication, and LDAP authentication.

Authorization: Spring Security offers a flexible and powerful authorization model that can be used to secure web applications.

Web Attacks: Spring Security provides protection against a wide range of web attacks, including cross-site scripting (XSS) and SQL injection attacks.

Spring Security is a very flexible framework that can be customized to meet the specific security needs of your application. In addition, Spring Security offers a number of features that are not available in other security frameworks.

One of the key features of Spring Security is its support for a wide range of authentication mechanisms. Spring Security supports both traditional authentication mechanisms, such as form-based authentication and HTTP basic authentication, and newer authentication mechanisms, such as LDAP authentication and token-based authentication.

Spring Security also offers a flexible authorization model that can be used to secure web applications. The authorization model supports both role-based access control and permission-based access control.

In addition, Spring Security provides protection against a wide range of web attacks. Spring Security offers protection against cross-site scripting (XSS) attacks, SQL injection attacks, and session hijacking attacks.

Spring Security is a very flexible framework that can be customized to meet the specific security needs of your application.

Integrating front-end frameworks with Spring Boot, such as Angular or React.

When it comes to integrating front-end frameworks with Spring Boot, there are a few things to keep in mind. First, you'll need to make sure that your front-end framework is compatible with the version of Spring Boot you're using. Second, you'll need to configure your build system to properly compile and package your front-end code. And finally, you'll need to configure Spring Boot to serve your front-end code.

Assuming you're using a compatible version of Angular or React, the next thing you'll need to do is configure your build system. With Angular, you'll need to use the Angular CLI to compile and package your code. With React, you'll need to use Webpack to compile and package your code. Once your code is compiled and packaged, you'll need to configure Spring Boot to serve it.

To do this, you'll need to add a ResourceHandler to your Spring Boot configuration. The

ResourceHandler will tell Spring Boot where to find your static files (i.e. your compiled and packaged front-end code). Once you've added the ResourceHandler, you'll need to add a Controller to map requests to your static files.

Assuming you're using Angular, your controller might look something like this:

```
@Controller public class MyController {
@RequestMapping("/") public String index() {
return "index.html"; } }
```

This controller will map requests to the root URL "/" to the "index.html" file in your static files directory.

Assuming you're using React, your controller might look something like this:

```
@Controller public class MyController {
@RequestMapping("/") public String index() {
return "index.html"; }
@RequestMapping("/{path}") public String
path(@PathVariable("path") String path) { return
path + ".html"; } }
```

This controller will map requests to the root URL "/" to the "index.html" file in your static files directory. It will also map requests to any other URL to a file with the same name in your static files directory.

Once you've added your ResourceHandler and Controller, you should be able to access your front-end code at the URL you've configured.

Chapter 4: Database Integration with Spring Boot

Working with relational databases in Spring Boot.

Spring Boot provides first-class support for working with relational databases. In this chapter, we will explore the different options that Spring Boot provides us for working with databases.

We will start by looking at how to configure a datasource. We will then look at how to use Spring Data JPA to work with our database. We will also look at how to use Spring Data JDBC to work with our database. Finally, we will look at how to use Spring Data REST to expose our data through a RESTful API.

Configuring and connecting to databases using Spring Data.

Spring Data provides comprehensive support for connecting to a wide variety of data sources, from relational databases such as MySQL, PostgreSQL, and Microsoft SQL Server to NoSQL databases such as MongoDB, Cassandra, and Redis.

Configuring a data source in Spring Data is a matter of defining a few properties in application.properties. For example, to connect to a MySQL database, you would need to specify the following properties:

```
spring.datasource.url=jdbc:mysql://localhost:3306/mydatabase
spring.datasource.username=myusername
spring.datasource.password=mypassword
```

Connecting to a database using Spring Data is a matter of creating a JdbcTemplate and passing it the data source. For example, to connect to a MySQL database, you would do the following:

```
JdbcTemplate jdbcTemplate = new JdbcTemplate(dataSource);
```

Once you have a JdbcTemplate, you can use it to query the database, update the database, and more.

Spring Data also provides support for more complex data access scenarios, such as using JPA to connect to a database. To use JPA with Spring Data, you need to configure a EntityManagerFactory. For example, to connect to a MySQL database, you would need to specify the following properties:

spring.jpa.database=MYSQL spring.jpa.database-platform=org.hibernate.dialect.MySQL5Dialect spring.jpa.show-sql=true

Once you have configured a EntityManagerFactory, you can use it to create a JpaTemplate. The JpaTemplate can then be used to query the database, update the database, and more.

Performing CRUD (Create, Read, Update, Delete) operations with Spring Boot.

Creating a Spring Boot application that performs CRUD operations on a database is a simple process. The first step is to create a new Spring Boot project and add the necessary dependencies. The next step is to configure the application to connect to the database. This can be done by adding a datasource configuration to the application.yml file. The last step is to create the controllers and services that will perform the CRUD operations.

The first step is to create a new Spring Boot project and add the necessary dependencies. The next step is to configure the application to connect to the database. This can be done by adding a datasource configuration to the application.yml file. The last step is to create the controllers and services that will perform the CRUD operations.

The first step is to create a new Spring Boot project and add the necessary dependencies. The next step is to configure the application to connect to the database. This can be done by adding a datasource configuration to the application.yml file. The last step is to create the controllers and services that will perform the CRUD operations.

The controllers will be responsible for handling the HTTP requests and responses. The services will be responsible for performing the actual CRUD operations.

Implementing data validation and constraints in Spring Boot.

Data validation is the process of ensuring that data is clean, correct, and useful. Data constraints are rules that limit or restrict the values that can be stored in a database.

Spring Boot provides several mechanisms for data validation and constraint enforcement. One way is to use the @Valid annotation on a controller method argument. This will cause Spring to validate the argument using the configured Validator (if any) and throw a MethodArgumentNotValidException if the validation fails.

Another way to enforce data constraints is to use the @Validated annotation on a controller class. This will cause Spring to validate all controller method arguments annotated with @Valid or @Validated .

Finally, data constraints can be enforced programmatically by implementing the Validator interface.

Utilizing Spring Data JPA for object-relational mapping.

Spring Data JPA is a framework that provides object-relational mapping between Java objects and relational databases. It is based on the Java Persistence API (JPA), which is a standard specification for accessing, persisting, and managing data in a Java EE application. Spring Data JPA is a part of the Spring Data project, which is an umbrella project that aims to provide support for new data access technologies, including NoSQL databases, map-reduce frameworks, and cloud-based data services.

Chapter 5: Building RESTful Services with Spring Boot

Implementing RESTful APIs using Spring Boot.

RESTful APIs are built on the principles of Representational State Transfer (REST), which is an architectural style for distributed systems. RESTful APIs are typically designed to work with HTTP, making them easy to use with the wide variety of HTTP clients and libraries available.

Spring Boot is a popular framework for building RESTful APIs. It is built on top of the Spring Framework and makes it easy to create stand-alone, production-grade Spring-based applications.

Spring Boot provides a number of features that make it easy to create and deploy RESTful APIs. For example, it can automatically configure a Jackson ObjectMapper for serialization and deserialization of JSON payloads. It also provides built-in support for many popular database technologies, making it easy to persist data.

In addition, Spring Boot provides a number of features to make it easy to test RESTful APIs. For example, it can automatically configure a RestTemplate for use with the test context. This makes it easy to test APIs without having to stand up a full application server.

To get started with Spring Boot, check out the Spring Boot Getting Started Guide.

Handling HTTP methods and request/response payloads in Spring Boot.

In Spring Boot, you can handle HTTP requests and responses in a number of ways. One way is to use the @RequestMapping annotation. This annotation can be used on a class or on a method.

If you use the @RequestMapping annotation on a class, all methods in that class will be mapped to the same URL. For example, if you have a class with two methods, one mapped to "/foo" and one mapped to "/bar", both methods will be accessible at "/foo" and "/bar".

If you use the @RequestMapping annotation on a method, that method will be mapped to the specified URL. For example, if you have a method mapped to "/foo", it will be accessible at "/foo".

The @RequestMapping annotation supports a number of request methods, including GET, POST, PUT, and DELETE. You can specify the request method in the annotation, or you can use the default request method, which is GET.

You can also specify the request and response payloads in the @RequestMapping annotation. The request payload is the data that is sent to the server in the request body. The response payload is the data that is sent back to the client in the response body.

Spring Boot also supports a number of other ways to handle HTTP requests and responses. For more information, see the Spring Boot documentation.

Implementing authentication and authorization with Spring Security.

Authentication is the process of verifying the identity of a user. Authorization is the process of determining what a user is allowed to do.

Spring Security is a framework that provides authentication and authorization services. It is easy to use and configure.

To implement authentication and authorization with Spring Security, you need to add the following dependencies to your project:

spring-security-core

spring-security-config

spring-security-web

You also need to configure Spring Security. The most basic configuration is to specify the URL patterns that should be secured and the roles that are required to access those URLs.

For example, to secure the URL pattern "/admin/**" so that only users with the role "ROLE_ADMIN" can access it, you would add the following configuration to your Spring Security configuration file:

```
<http>

<intercept-url pattern="/admin/**"
access="ROLE_ADMIN"/>

</http>
```

You can also secure individual methods by annotating them with the @PreAuthorize or @PostAuthorize annotations.

For example, to secure the method "getUserById" so that it can only be accessed by users with the role "ROLE_ADMIN", you would annotate it as follows:

```
@PreAuthorize("hasRole('ROLE_ADMIN')")

public User getUserById(Long id) {

// ...

}
```

Utilizing Spring Boot's support for HATEOAS (Hypermedia as the Engine of Application State).

In Chapter 5, Building RESTful Services with Spring Boot, the author covers Spring Boot's support for HATEOAS (Hypermedia as the Engine of Application State).

HATEOAS is a constraint of the REST application architecture that keeps the RESTful style architecture unique from most other network application architectures. The term "hypermedia" refers to the fact that a RESTful application exposes its data and functionality as a set of resources that can be linked together. A client of a RESTful application can navigate through the application by following the links exposed by the server.

The author gives the example of a simple blog application. A client can navigate to the home page of the blog, which contains links to the individual blog posts. The client can then choose to follow a link to a specific blog post.

The author also covers Spring Boot's support for content negotiation. Content negotiation is the process of selecting the best representation for a given resource. Spring Boot supports content negotiation by default and will select the best representation based on the Accept header of the request.

The author concludes with a discussion of error handling in RESTful applications. Spring Boot provides a @RestControllerAdvice annotation that can be used to global error handling for a RESTful application.

Versioning and documenting RESTful APIs with Spring Boot.

Versioning and documenting RESTful APIs with Spring Boot is a process of keeping track of changes made to a REST API over time. This is important so that developers can keep track of what has changed, and so that users can understand how to use the latest version of the API.

Spring Boot makes it easy to version and document RESTful APIs. To version an API, simply add a version number to the end of the URL. For example, to version the API at http://example.com/api, you would add a version number like http://example.com/api/v1.

Documenting an API is just as easy. Spring Boot automatically generates documentation for RESTful APIs. This documentation includes information on the URL structure, the parameters that can be passed to the API, and the response format.

Chapter 6: Data Validation and Error Handling in Spring Boot

Validating request data using Spring Boot's validation framework.

When using Spring Boot's validation framework, request data can be validated in a number of ways. One way is to use the @Valid annotation on a controller method. This will cause Spring to validate the request data before invoking the method. Another way is to use the Validator interface. This can be used to validate request data in a more custom way.

Handling and customizing validation errors in Spring Boot.

When it comes to validation in Spring Boot, there are a few different ways to go about it. You can either use the built-in validation features of Spring Boot, or you can create your own custom validation rules.

If you want to use the built-in validation features of Spring Boot, there are a few different ways to go about it. You can either use the @Valid annotation on your controller methods, or you can use the Validator interface.

If you want to use the @Valid annotation, you can simply add it to your controller method parameters. Spring Boot will then automatically validate the parameters before invoking the method.

If you want to use the Validator interface, you can create a class that implements the interface and then add it to your Spring context. Spring Boot will then automatically use your validator when validating parameters.

You can also create your own custom validation rules by creating a class that implements the ConstraintValidator interface. Spring Boot will then automatically use your validator when validating parameters.

If you want to customize the way Spring Boot handles validation errors, you can do so by creating a class that implements the ErrorHandler interface. Spring Boot will then use your custom error handler when there are validation errors.

Implementing global exception handling and error responses in Spring Boot.

Spring Boot provides a number of features for handling exceptions and errors. By default, if a Exception is thrown from a controller, Spring Boot will respond with a 500 Internal Server Error status code. However, you can also configure Spring Boot to return a custom error response.

To configure a global exception handler, you can create a class that implements the HandlerExceptionResolver interface. This class can then be registered with the Spring Boot application.

When an exception is thrown, the HandlerExceptionResolver will be invoked and can generate a response with the appropriate status code and message.

For example, you might want to return a 400 Bad Request status code if a validation error occurs. You can do this by checking for the presence of a BindingResult in the exception handler method. If a BindingResult is found, you can check if there are any errors and return a 400 status code if there are.

You can also use the @ControllerAdvice annotation to create a global exception handler. This annotation can be used on a class that contains exception handler methods. These methods can then be used to generate responses for any exceptions that occur in the application.

The @ExceptionHandler annotation can be used on a method to handle a specific type of exception. For example, you might want to handle ValidationException s differently than other exceptions.

You can also use the @RestControllerAdvice annotation to create a global exception handler for REST controllers. This annotation will cause any exception that is thrown from a controller method to be handled by the exception handler methods.

Spring Boot also provides a number of properties that can be used to configure how exceptions and errors are handled. For example, you can use the server.error.whitelabel.enabled property to enable the whitelabel error page. This page will be displayed for any unhandled exception.

You can also use the server.error.path property to configure a custom error path. This path will be used to generate the response for any unhandled exception.

Finally, you can use the server.error.include-stacktrace property to include the stack trace in the error response. This can be useful for debugging purposes.

Utilizing custom exception handlers and error handling strategies in Spring Boot.

Spring Boot provides a number of features that can be used to handle errors and exceptions in a web application. One of the most useful features is the ability to create custom exception handlers.

Exception handlers allow you to map an exception to a specific response. For example, you could map a DataAccessException to an HTTP status code of 500. This is particularly useful for handling errors that are not necessarily caused by user input, such as database connection errors.

Another useful feature is the ability to map specific errors to specific responses. This is useful for handling errors that are caused by user input, such as validation errors.

Error handling strategies can be used to control how errors are handled in a web application. There are a number of different strategies that can be used, and the choice of strategy will depend on the specific requirements of the application.

One common strategy is to use a global error handler. This is a single place where all errors are handled. The advantage of this approach is that it is simple to implement and maintain. The disadvantage is that it can be difficult to debug errors, as all errors are handled in the same place.

Another common strategy is to use per-controller error handlers. This means that each controller has its own error handler. The advantage of this approach is that it is easier to debug errors, as each controller has its own error handler. The disadvantage is that it can be more difficult to maintain, as each controller must be updated if the error handling needs to be changed.

A third common strategy is to use a combination of global and per-controller error handlers. This means that some errors are handled globally, while others are handled by specific controllers. The advantage of this approach is that it combines the simplicity of the global approach with the flexibility of the per-controller approach. The disadvantage is that it can be more difficult to debug errors, as some errors are handled in multiple places.

Spring Boot provides a number of other features that can be used to handle errors and exceptions in a web application. These include the ability to log errors, the ability to send email notifications, and the ability to redirect users to a specific page.

Logging and monitoring errors in Spring Boot applications.

Logging and monitoring errors in Spring Boot applications is a critical part of ensuring the stability and health of the application. There are a few different ways to approach this, but the most important thing is to have a clear understanding of what errors are being logged and why they are happening.

One way to approach this is to use a tool like Spring Boot Admin, which provides a web interface for viewing application logs. This can be useful for quickly identifying and fixing errors. Another approach is to use a logging framework like Log4j, which provides more granular control over what is logged and how it is displayed.

Whatever approach is used, it is important to make sure that errors are being logged to a central location so that they can be easily monitored and investigated. Additionally, it is often helpful to setup alerts so that you are notified immediately when an error occurs.

Chapter 7: Caching and Performance Optimization in Spring Boot

Utilizing Spring Boot's caching mechanisms for improved performance.

Spring Boot provides a number of caching mechanisms that can be used to improve performance. The most common mechanism is the use of a cache manager, which is a component that manages the caching of data in Spring Boot applications.

The cache manager is responsible for creating and managing the cache, as well as providing methods for accessing and storing data in the cache. Spring Boot provides a number of cache managers, which can be configured using the spring.cache.type property.

The most common cache manager is the SimpleCacheManager, which is a basic cache manager that can be used for most applications. The SimpleCacheManager supports a number of caching strategies, including the use of a LRU cache, which is a type of cache that stores the most recently used data.

Another caching mechanism that can be used in Spring Boot applications is the use of a EhCache cache manager. EhCache is a more sophisticated cache manager that supports a number of features, including the ability to cluster caches.

In order to use EhCache, you must first add the EhCache dependency to your application. Once the dependency has been added, you can configure the EhCache cache manager using the spring.cache.type property.

Once the cache manager has been configured, you can then configure the cache itself. The cache can be configured using the spring.cache.cache-names property. This property defines the name of the cache, as well as the type of data that will be cached.

The cache can also be configured to use a specific eviction policy. The eviction policy is responsible for removing data from the cache when it is no longer needed. The most common eviction policy is the LRU policy, which removes the least recently used data from the cache.

Once the cache has been configured, you can then access the data in the cache using the cache manager. The cache manager provides a number of methods for accessing the data in the cache, including the get() and put() methods.

The get() method is used to retrieve data from the cache, while the put() method is used to store data in the cache. In order to use the cache manager, you must first obtain a reference to the cache. This can be done using the @Autowired annotation.

Once you have a reference to the cache, you can then use the cache manager to access the data in the cache. The cache manager provides a number of methods for accessing the data in the cache, including the get() and put() methods.

Configuring caching providers, such as Redis or Ehcache in Spring Boot.

Caching is a technique that can be used to improve the performance of a web application by storing data in memory so that it can be quickly accessed the next time the same data is requested.

There are a number of caching providers available, such as Redis and Ehcache. In Spring Boot, you can configure a caching provider by setting the spring.cache.type property in your application.properties file.

For example, to configure Redis as your caching provider, you would add the following to your application.properties file:

```
spring.cache.type=redis
```

You will also need to add a dependency on the Redis driver to your project. For example, if you are using Maven, you would add the following to your pom.xml file:

```xml
<dependency>

<groupId>org.springframework.boot</groupId>

<artifactId>spring-boot-starter-data-redis</artifactId>

</dependency>
```

Once you have configured a caching provider, you can enable caching by annotating your methods with the @Cacheable annotation. For example:

```java
@Cacheable("books")

public Book getBookById(long id) {

// ...

}
```

This will cause the getBookById() method to be cached, using the "books" cache. The next time this method is invoked, the cached data will be returned, instead of executing the method body.

You can also annotate methods with the @CacheEvict annotation to remove data from the cache. For example:

```
@CacheEvict("books")

public void deleteBookById(long id) {

// ...

}
```

This will cause the book with the given id to be removed from the "books" cache.

You can also use the @Caching annotation to annotate a method with multiple caching annotations. For example:

```
@Caching(

cacheable = { @Cacheable("books") },
```

```
evict = { @CacheEvict("books") }
)
public Book updateBookById(long id, Book book) {
// ...
}
```

This will cause the book with the given id to be
cached in the "books" cache, and then evicted from
the cache after the method has been executed.

Caching strategies and best practices for different use cases in Spring Boot.

There are many caching strategies and best
practices for different use cases in Spring Boot.
However, some of the most common and
important ones are listed below:

1. Use an in-memory cache for frequently accessed
data: In-memory caching can be extremely helpful
in increasing the performance of Spring Boot
applications. It can be used to store frequently
accessed data in memory, so that it can be quickly
accessed by the application when needed.

2. Use a disk-based cache for data that is not frequently accessed: Disk-based caching can be used for data that is not frequently accessed by the application. This can help to improve performance by avoiding the need to retrieve this data from a remote location every time it is needed.

3. Use a cache for data that is expensive to generate: Caching can also be used for data that is expensive to generate. For example, if an application needs to retrieve data from a database every time it is needed, it can be helpful to cache this data so that it does not need to be retrieved from the database each time.

4. Use a cache to avoid retrieving data that is not needed: Caching can also be used to avoid retrieving data that is not needed by the application. For example, if an application only needs to retrieve data that has been changed since the last time it was retrieved, it can be helpful to cache this data so that it does not need to be retrieved unnecessarily.

5. Use a cache to improve the performance of batch operations: Caching can also be used to improve the performance of batch operations. For example, if an application needs to retrieve data from a database in order to process it, it can be helpful to cache this data so that it does not need to be

retrieved from the database each time the batch operation is run.

Implementing performance optimizations, such as lazy loading and caching of expensive operations in Spring Boot.

Lazy loading is a technique for loading data on demand. This can be useful for reducing the amount of time and resources required to load a large data set.

Caching is a technique for storing data in a temporary location so that it can be quickly accessed. This can be useful for reducing the amount of time and resources required to retrieve data from a database or other slow resource.

Both of these techniques can be used to improve the performance of a Spring Boot application.

Monitoring and analyzing application performance using Spring Boot Actuator.

Spring Boot Actuator is a sub-project of Spring Boot that provides production-ready features such as monitoring and analyzing application performance. It also provides a set of tools to help you manage and monitor your Spring Boot-based application in production.

Some of the features of Spring Boot Actuator include:

1. Monitoring application performance: Spring Boot Actuator can help you monitor your application's performance by providing information on request handling times, database query times, and so on.

2. Analyzing application performance: Spring Boot Actuator can help you analyze your application's performance by providing information on request handling times, database query times, and so on.

3. Managing and monitoring your Spring Boot-based application: Spring Boot Actuator provides a set of tools to help you manage and monitor your Spring Boot-based application in production.

4. Enabling and disabling features: Spring Boot Actuator can help you enable and disable features of your application, such as monitoring, caching, and so on.

5. Changing configuration: Spring Boot Actuator can help you change the configuration of your application, such as the logging level, cache size, and so on.

Chapter 8: Authentication and Authorization in Spring Boot

Implementing user authentication and authorization using Spring Security.

User authentication is the process of verifying a user's identity. This can be done in a number of ways, but the most common is to use a username and password. Once a user has been authenticated, they will need to be authorized to access the resources they are requesting.

Spring Security is a framework that provides user authentication and authorization services. It is built on top of the Java Authentication and Authorization Service (JAAS) and the Java Security Manager. Spring Security can be used to secure web applications, RESTful services, and even command-line applications.

When configuring Spring Security, you will need to specify the authentication and authorization rules for your application. These rules can be configured in a number of ways, but the most common is to use an XML configuration file.

Once the Spring Security configuration is in place, users will be able to authenticate and authorize themselves by using the provided username and password. Spring Security will then use the configured rules to determine whether or not the user is allowed to access the requested resource.

Configuring authentication providers, such as databases or LDAP in Spring Boot.

When configuring authentication providers in Spring Boot, there are a few things to keep in mind. First, you will need to configure the authentication provider itself. This can be done by specifying the class name of the authentication provider in the application.properties file. For example, if you are using a database-based authentication provider, you would specify the class name as follows:

```
spring.security.authentication.provider.class=org.springframework.security.authentication.dao.DaoAuthenticationProvider
```

Next, you will need to configure the details of the authentication provider. This will include specifying the data source that the authentication provider will use, as well as the SQL query that will be used to retrieve the user's credentials. For example, if you are using a MySQL database, you would configure the authentication provider as follows:

```
spring.security.authentication.provider.dao.data-source=jdbc:mysql://localhost:3306/mydatabase
spring.security.authentication.provider.dao.sql=SELECT username, password FROM users WHERE username=?
```

Finally, you will need to configure the authentication manager. This can be done by specifying the authentication manager class in the application.properties file. For example, if you are using the default authentication manager, you would specify the class name as follows:

```
spring.security.authentication.manager.class=org.springframework.security.authentication.ProviderManager
```

Once you have configured the authentication manager, you will need to specify the authentication providers that it will use. This can be done by specifying a list of authentication providers in the application.properties file. For example, if you are using the database-based authentication provider and the LDAP-based authentication provider, you would specify the authentication providers as follows:

```
spring.security.authentication.manager.providers=
org.springframework.security.authentication.dao.
DaoAuthenticationProvider,
org.springframework.security.authentication.ldap.
LdapAuthenticationProvider
```

After you have configured the authentication providers, you will need to specify the order in which they will be used. This can be done by specifying the order in which the authentication providers will be used in the application.properties file. For example, if you want the database-based authentication provider to be used first, and the LDAP-based authentication provider to be used second, you would specify the order as follows:

```
spring.security.authentication.manager.order=1,2
```

Once you have configured the authentication providers and the authentication manager, you will need to configure the security filter chain. This can be done by specifying the security filter chain in the application.properties file. For example, if you are using the default security filter chain, you would specify the filter chain as follows:

spring.security.filter-chain=default

After you have configured the security filter chain, you will need to specify the security filters that will be used. This can be done by specifying a list of security filters in the application.properties file. For example, if you are using the database-based authentication provider and the LDAP-based authentication provider, you would specify the security filters as follows:

spring.security.filter-chain.filters=org.springframework.security.web.authentication.preauth.PreAuthenticatedAuthenticationFilter,

org.springframework.security.web.authentication.
www.BasicAuthenticationFilter

After you have configured the security filters, you
will need to specify the order in which they will be
used. This can be done by specifying the order in
which the security filters will be used in the
application.properties file. For example, if you
want the database-based authentication filter to be
used first, and the LDAP-based authentication
filter to be used second, you would specify the
order as follows:

spring.security.filter-chain.order=1,2

Finally, you will need to configure the
authentication success handler. This can be done
by specifying the authentication success handler
class in the application.properties file. For
example, if you are using the default
authentication success handler, you would specify
the class name as follows:

```
spring.security.authentication.success-
handler=org.springframework.security.web.authe
ntication.SimpleUrlAuthenticationSuccessHandler
```

After you have configured the authentication
success handler, you will need to specify the
authentication success URL. This can be done by
specifying the authentication success URL in the
application.properties file. For example, if you
want the authentication success URL to be
/loginSuccess, you would specify the URL as
follows:

```
spring.security.authentication.success-
handler.default-target-url=/loginSuccess
```

Role-based and permission-based access control in Spring Boot.

In a Spring Boot application, role-based and
permission-based access control can be
implemented using the @PreAuthorize and
@PostAuthorize annotations.

@PreAuthorize is used to restrict access to a method based on the user's role. For example, the following code would allow only users with the role of "ADMIN" to access the method:

@PreAuthorize("hasRole('ADMIN')") public void someMethod() { // Code here }

@PostAuthorize is used to check if a user has the required permissions to access a method. For example, the following code would allow only users with the "READ" permission to access the method:

@PostAuthorize("hasPermission('READ')") public void someMethod() { // Code here }

Implementing OAuth 2.0 for secure API authentication and authorization in Spring Boot.

OAuth 2.0 is an authorization protocol that enables applications to obtain limited access to user accounts on an HTTP service. It works by delegating user authentication to the service that hosts the user account, and authorizing third-party applications to access the user account. OAuth 2.0

provides a way to grant limited access to user accounts without giving away the user's password.

In order to implement OAuth 2.0 in Spring Boot, we need to first add the spring-security-oauth2 dependency to our project.

```
<dependency>

<groupId>org.springframework.security.oauth</groupId>

<artifactId>spring-security-oauth2</artifactId>

<version>2.3.4.RELEASE</version>

</dependency>
```

We also need to configure our application to use OAuth 2.0. This can be done by adding the following to our application.properties file:

```
security.oauth2.client.client-id=your-client-id

security.oauth2.client.client-secret=your-client-secret
```

security.oauth2.client.authorized-grant-
types=password,refresh_token

security.oauth2.client.scope=read,write

security.oauth2.resource.user-info-
uri=https://example.com/user

With these configurations in place, we can now
create a controller that will handle the
authorization code flow.

```
@RestController

@RequestMapping("/oauth")

public class OAuthController {

@Autowired

private OAuth2RestTemplate
oauth2RestTemplate;

@GetMapping("/user")

public Map<String, Object> getUserInfo() {

return
oauth2RestTemplate.getForObject("https://examp
le.com/user", Map.class);
```

```
    }

}
```

In this controller, we are using the OAuth2RestTemplate to make a request to the resource server to get the user's information. The resource server will return a JSON object that contains the user's information.

Utilizing JSON Web Tokens (JWT) for stateless authentication in Spring Boot.

JSON Web Tokens, or JWTs, are a type of token that can be used to authenticate users on a stateless, decentralized system. JWTs are typically used in conjunction with a centralized authentication server, such as an OAuth provider. When a user authenticates with the authentication server, they are issued a JWT. The JWT can then be used to make requests to other services on the system, without the need to re-authenticate with the authentication server.

JWTs have a few advantages over other types of tokens. First, they are very compact, so they can be easily passed around in headers or query parameters. Second, they are self-contained, so all the information needed to authenticate a user is included in the token itself. This means that JWTs can be used on systems where the authentication server is not accessible, or where communication between services is not possible.

There are a few drawbacks to JWTs as well. First, they are not as secure as other types of tokens, since they are not encrypted. This means that if a JWT is intercepted, the contents can be read by anyone. Second, JWTs can be forged, so it is possible for a malicious user to create a fake JWT and gain access to a system.

In order to use JWTs for authentication in Spring Boot, you will need to add the spring-security-jwt dependency to your project. Once you have done that, you can configure Spring Security to use JWTs by setting the authenticationManager.authenticationProvider.jwt .enabled property to true in your application.properties file.

Once you have done that, you can create a JWT AuthenticationFilter that will extract the JWT from the request and attempt to authenticate the user. If the user is successfully authenticated, a SecurityContext will be created and populated with the user's details. The SecurityContext will then be used by Spring Security to make decisions about what the user is allowed to do.

Here is an example of a JWT AuthenticationFilter:

```
@Component

public class JWTAuthenticationFilter extends
OncePerRequestFilter { @Override protected void
doFilterInternal(HttpServletRequest request,
HttpServletResponse response, FilterChain
filterChain) throws ServletException, IOException
{ String header =
request.getHeader("Authorization"); if (header ==
null || !header.startsWith("Bearer ")) { throw new
JwtException("No JWT token found in request
headers"); } String token = header.substring(7);
try { JwtParser jwtParser =
Jwts.parser().setSigningKey("secret");
Jws<Claims> jws =
jwtParser.parseClaimsJws(token); String
username = jws.getBody().getSubject();
List<String> roles = jws.getBody().get("roles",
List.class); if (username == null) { throw new
JwtException("JWT token does not contain a
username"); } if (roles == null || roles.isEmpty()) {
throw new JwtException("JWT token does not
contain any roles"); }
UsernamePasswordAuthenticationToken
```

```
authentication = new
UsernamePasswordAuthenticationToken(usernam
e, null,
roles.stream().map(SimpleGrantedAuthority::new
).collect(Collectors.toList()));
SecurityContextHolder.getContext().setAuthentica
tion(authentication); } catch (JwtException e) {
response.sendError(HttpServletResponse.SC_UNA
UTHORIZED, "Invalid JWT token"); return; }
filterChain.doFilter(request, response); } }
```

Chapter 9: Testing Spring Boot Applications

Introduction to testing methodologies in Spring Boot.

Testing is a process of verifying the correctness of a software program. There are many different methodologies for testing, each with its own advantages and disadvantages.

The most common testing methodologies are unit testing, integration testing, and system testing. Unit testing is the process of testing individual units of code, such as classes and methods. Integration testing is the process of testing how different units of code work together. System testing is the process of testing an entire system, such as a web application.

Spring Boot provides a number of features that make it easy to write unit tests, integration tests, and system tests. For example, Spring Boot provides an in-memory database that can be used for unit testing. Spring Boot also provides a test runner that makes it easy to run tests.

In addition to the built-in features, there are a number of third-party libraries that can be used for testing Spring Boot applications. For example, the JUnit library provides a number of features that make it easy to write unit tests. The Spring TestContext Framework provides a number of features that make it easy to write integration tests.

Testing is an important part of developing software applications. Spring Boot makes it easy to write well-designed tests.

Writing unit tests and integration tests for Spring Boot applications.

Spring Boot provides a number of features that can be used to write unit tests and integration tests for Spring Boot applications.

One of the most important features is the ability to use the @SpringBootTest annotation to load a Spring ApplicationContext for unit tests. This annotation can be used to load a specific configuration for the test, or to load the full Spring Boot application.

Spring Boot also provides a number of test utilities that can be used to write unit tests and integration tests. These utilities include the TestRestTemplate, which can be used to make HTTP requests to a

Spring Boot application, and the MockMvc, which can be used to test a Spring MVC application.

In addition, Spring Boot provides a number of features that can be used to write unit tests and integration tests for Spring Boot applications. One of the most important features is the ability to use the @SpringBootTest annotation to load a Spring ApplicationContext for unit tests. This annotation can be used to load a specific configuration for the test, or to load the full Spring Boot application.

Spring Boot also provides a number of test utilities that can be used to write unit tests and integration tests. These utilities include the TestRestTemplate, which can be used to make HTTP requests to a Spring Boot application, and the MockMvc, which can be used to test a Spring MVC application.

Utilizing testing frameworks, such as JUnit and Mockito for Spring Boot applications.

The Spring Framework is a powerful tool for helping developers write high-quality code. One of the most important aspects of writing high-quality code is writing comprehensive tests. Tests help ensure that your code is correct and that it behaves as expected.

There are many different testing frameworks available for Java, but two of the most popular are JUnit and Mockito. These frameworks can be used to test Spring Boot applications.

JUnit is a popular unit testing framework. Unit tests are tests that focus on a small, specific unit of code. In the context of a Spring Boot application, a unit might be a single method in a service class. JUnit can be used to write tests that verify that a method behaves as expected.

Mockito is a popular mocking framework. Mocking is a technique that can be used to stub out or mock out parts of an application. This is useful when you want to test a specific component of an application without needing to depend on other components. For example, you might want to mock out a database repository so that you can test your service layer without needing to connect to a real database.

Both JUnit and Mockito are powerful tools that can be used to write comprehensive tests for Spring Boot applications.

Testing Spring MVC controllers and RESTful APIs for Spring Boot applications.

Testing Spring MVC controllers and RESTful APIs for Spring Boot applications can be done using the Spring MVC Test Framework and the RestTemplate class.

The Spring MVC Test Framework can be used to test Spring MVC controllers by setting up mock requests and responses, and by injecting test data into the controller. The RestTemplate class can be used to test RESTful APIs by making HTTP requests and checking the response.

To test a Spring MVC controller, you can use the @WebMvcTest annotation. This annotation will setup a Spring MVC context and can be used to inject mock objects into the controller.

To test a RESTful API, you can use the RestTemplate class to make HTTP requests and check the response. You can also use the @MockRestServiceServer annotation to mock out the RestTemplate class.

Testing database interactions and using test doubles for Spring Boot applications.

Database interactions are a critical part of any application, and Spring Boot applications are no different. Testing these interactions can be difficult, as there are many moving parts involved. In addition, database interactions often have side effects that can impact the rest of the application.

One way to simplify testing database interactions is to use test doubles. Test doubles are dummy objects that stand in for real objects during testing. By using test doubles, we can isolate the database interactions and test them in isolation from the rest of the application.

There are many different types of test doubles, but the most common type is the mock object. Mock objects are created by a mocking framework, such as Mockito. Mockito allows us to create mock objects and stub out methods on those objects. When a method on a mock object is invoked, we can specify what should happen. This allows us to test the interaction without actually hitting the database.

Another type of test double is the stub. Stubs are similar to mock objects, but they are usually hand-coded. Stubs typically return hard-coded values, so they are useful for testing simple interactions.

Finally, there are also fake objects. Fake objects are actual implementations of the object being tested, but they use in-memory data stores instead of hitting the database. This can be useful for testing complex interactions.

In general, it is best to use the simplest test double that will get the job done. Mock objects are usually the best choice, but stubs and fake objects can be used in certain situations.

When testing database interactions, it is important to pay attention to any side effects that might occur. For example, if a database insert operation also triggers a cache invalidation, then the test should verify that the cache is invalidated. Otherwise, the test might pass even though the application is not working correctly.

It is also important to think about how the database will be reset between test runs. In most cases, it is best to use an in-memory database for testing. This way, the database can be easily reset between test runs. If an actual database is being used, then care must be taken to ensure that the data is reset properly.

In summary, testing database interactions can be difficult. However, by using test doubles and paying attention to side effects, it is possible to write comprehensive tests for these interactions.

Chapter 10: Building Microservices with Spring Boot

Introduction to microservices architecture and its benefits.

Microservices are a type of software architecture that decomposes a application into smaller, independent services that communicate with each other.

The benefits of using a microservices architecture include:

1. Increased flexibility and scalability: Because each microservice is independent, it can be scaled up or down as needed without affecting the other services.

2. Improved fault tolerance: If one microservice goes down, the others can continue to run without interruption.

3. easier to develop and deploy: Each microservice can be developed and deployed independently, which makes the overall process simpler and faster.

4. improved maintainability: Since each microservice is independent, it is easier to maintain and update each one separately.

Designing and implementing microservices using Spring Boot.

Microservices are a type of software architecture that allows for the development of individual components of a larger application as separate, independent services. These services are typically small, self-contained, and can be deployed and updated independently of each other.

Spring Boot is a popular framework for developing microservices. It provides a number of features that make it easy to develop and deploy microservices, including:

- Automatic configuration: Spring Boot can automatically configure a microservice based on its dependencies. This eliminates the need for manual configuration and makes it easy to deploy new versions of a microservice without affecting other services.

- Embedded server: Spring Boot comes with an embedded server, which makes it easy to deploy a microservice without the need to install and configure a separate server.

- Health check: Spring Boot includes a health check endpoint that can be used to check the health of a microservice. This can be used to monitor the health of a service, and to identify and diagnose problems.

- Management endpoints: Spring Boot includes a number of management endpoints that can be used to monitor and manage a microservice. These endpoints can be used to view information about the service, such as its dependencies, configuration, and health.

Service discovery and communication between microservices in Spring Boot.

Service discovery is a key component of a microservices architecture. It allows services to find and communicate with each other, and it is a key enabler of resilience and scalability.

Spring Boot includes a number of features that make it easy to build microservices that use service discovery. For example, it can automatically register your microservice with a service registry, and it can provide a client-side load balancer that uses the service registry to lookup and route requests to the appropriate service instance.

In addition, Spring Boot provides a number of communication mechanisms that can be used between microservices, including HTTP, REST, and messaging protocols such as AMQP.

Implementing fault tolerance and resilience in microservices in Spring Boot.

Microservices are inherently fault-tolerant and resilient due to their distributed nature. However, there are certain design patterns and practices that can be used to further improve the fault tolerance and resilience of microservices.

One common pattern is the use of circuit breakers. A circuit breaker is used to prevent cascading failures by breaking the connection between services when an error is detected. This allows the rest of the system to continue functioning while the failing service is isolated and fixed.

Another common pattern is the use of bulkheads. Bulkheads are used to isolate different parts of the system so that a failure in one part does not affect the other parts. This is especially important in microservices systems where each service is typically responsible for a single task.

Finally, it is important to design microservices with failure in mind. This means designing services that can gracefully handle failures and degrade gracefully when necessary. It also means designing for recovery, so that failed services can be automatically restarted or replaced.

All of these patterns and practices can be implemented in Spring Boot applications using the various Spring Boot starters and libraries. For example, the Spring Cloud Netflix project provides starters and libraries for circuit breakers, bulkheads, and other resilience patterns.

Deploying and scaling microservices with Spring Cloud.

Microservices are an architectural style that structures an application as a collection of small, independent services that communicate with each other. They are built around the business capabilities of the application and are independently deployable and scalable.

Spring Cloud is a set of tools for microservices development on the Spring Platform. It provides a library of connectors for various cloud providers, and a set of tools for implementing common microservices patterns such as service discovery, circuit breakers, and distributed tracing.

To deploy and scale microservices with Spring Cloud, you need to first create a Spring Boot application and add the necessary dependencies for the Spring Cloud components you want to use. For example, to use service discovery with Eureka, you would add the spring-cloud-starter-eureka dependency.

Once you have your application set up, you can then deploy it to a cloud provider. Spring Cloud provides connectors for various cloud providers, such as Cloud Foundry, Amazon Web Services, and Heroku.

To scale your application, you can use the Spring Cloud Scaleout library. This library provides a set of tools for horizontally scaling Spring Boot applications. For example, you can use the Spring Cloud Scaleout ZooKeeper recipe to scale your

application by adding new instances of your
application to a ZooKeeper ensemble.

Chapter 11: Deployment and DevOps with Spring Boot

Packaging and deploying Spring Boot applications.

Spring Boot makes it easy to create stand-alone, production-grade Spring-based Applications that you can "just run". We take an opinionated view of the Spring platform and third-party libraries so you can get started with minimum fuss. Most Spring Boot applications need very little Spring configuration.

You can use Spring Boot in the same way as any other Java application. We've provided a few example applications that you can run as is. You can also use Spring Boot to create your own WAR file.

When you are ready to deploy your Spring Boot application, you have a few options. You can deploy it to an existing application server, or you can use Spring Boot's embedded servers.

If you want to deploy your Spring Boot application to an existing application server, you will need to create a traditional WAR file. Spring Boot includes support for creating WAR files. You can use the spring-boot-starter-tomcat starter to add Tomcat as an embedded server to your application.

If you want to deploy your application to an embedded server, you can use the spring-boot-starter-jetty or spring-boot-starter-undertow starters. These starters add Jetty or Undertow as the embedded server to your application.

When you package your application as a WAR file, you can use any of the embedded servers. The embedded server will be started and will manage your application and its dependencies.

You can also use the spring-boot-maven-plugin to package your application as an executable JAR file. This file can be run with java -jar. The plugin will package your application and its dependencies into a single JAR file. It will also autoconfigure an embedded server to run your application.

If you want to deploy your application to an external application server, you will need to package it as a traditional WAR file. You can use the spring-boot-starter-tomcat starter to add Tomcat as an embedded server to your application.

When you deploy your application to an external application server, the server will manage your application and its dependencies.

Configuring production-ready features with Spring Boot Actuator.

Spring Boot Actuator is a sub-project of Spring Boot that provides production-ready features for monitoring and managing Spring Boot applications. It includes a number of built-in endpoints that can be used for monitoring and managing your application.

You can use the Actuator endpoint to configure your application for production-ready features. For example, you can use the endpoints to:

- Configure logging levels for your application
- Configure health check settings
- Enable or disable features
- View application metrics
- View application trace information

The Actuator endpoint is also a great way to get started with monitoring and managing your Spring Boot application. You can use the built-in endpoints to get started, and then add your own custom endpoints as needed.

Utilizing containerization technologies, such as Docker, for Spring Boot applications.

Containerization is a process of packaging an application along with its dependencies, libraries, and configuration files into a self-contained unit called a container. This enables the application to run smoothly and predictably in different environments, such as on-premises servers, virtual machines, and cloud platforms.

Docker is a popular containerization platform that allows developers to package their applications into self-contained units called "Docker containers." Docker containers can be run on any platform that supports the Docker runtime, such as on-premises servers, virtual machines, and cloud platforms.

Spring Boot is a Java-based framework that makes it easy to create stand-alone, production-grade Spring-based applications that can be run in any environment, including in Docker containers.

There are many benefits to using containerization technologies, such as Docker, for Spring Boot applications. Containerization allows for consistent and reliable deployments of Spring Boot applications in different environments. Containers also provide isolation and security benefits, as each container runs in its own isolated environment and can be configured with its own security settings.

In addition, containers can be used to create portable and reproducible development environments. For example, a developer can create a Docker container that contains all the necessary dependencies, libraries, and configuration files for their Spring Boot application. This container can then be used by other developers on their own machines to develop and test the application.

Overall, using containerization technologies, such as Docker, for Spring Boot applications can provide many benefits, including consistent and reliable deployments, isolation and security benefits, and the ability to create portable and reproducible development environments.

Continuous integration and deployment (CI/CD) with Spring Boot.

Continuous integration (CI) is a development practice that requires developers to integrate code into a shared repository several times a day. Each check-in is then verified by an automated build, allowing teams to detect problems early.

Continuous deployment (CD) takes CI one step further, by automatically deploying the application to a production server after each successful build. This allows for rapid feedback and reduces the risk of human error in the deployment process.

Spring Boot makes it easy to set up a CI/CD pipeline for your application. There are a number of open source tools that can be used, such as Jenkins, Travis CI, or CircleCI.

Once you have set up your CI/CD pipeline, you can simply commit your code changes and let the pipeline take care of the rest. Your application will be built, tested, and deployed automatically, with minimal effort on your part.

Monitoring and logging Spring Boot applications in production.

Monitoring and logging are important aspects of any production application. Spring Boot provides a number of features to help you monitor and log your application in production.

Spring Boot uses the Commons Logging library by default for logging. This library provides a number of features to help you configure and manage your logs.

You can use the Spring Boot Admin project to monitor your Spring Boot application in production. Spring Boot Admin is a web-based application that provides a number of features for monitoring and managing Spring Boot applications.

You can also use the Spring Boot Actuator project to monitor and manage your Spring Boot application in production. Spring Boot Actuator provides a number of features for monitoring and managing your application.

Chapter 12: Best Practices and Advanced Topics in Spring Boot

Implementing security best practices in Spring Boot applications.

When it comes to securing Spring Boot applications, there are a number of best practices that should be followed. First and foremost, it is important to keep the application up to date with the latest security patches. Spring Boot applications should also be configured to use secure protocols such as HTTPS and TLS. Furthermore, it is important to use strong authentication and authorization measures. Finally, it is also important to monitor the application for any security issues.

Optimizing Spring Boot applications for scalability and performance.

When it comes to optimizing Spring Boot applications for scalability and performance, there are a few key areas to focus on.

One area that is often overlooked is the application's startup time. A slow startup time can be a major bottleneck, especially in a microservices environment where each application is started independently. There are a few things that can be done to speed up startup time, such as using a lightweight application server, reducing the number of dependencies, and using lazy initialization where possible.

Another area to focus on is the application's memory footprint. A large memory footprint can lead to OutOfMemoryErrors and can also make the application more difficult to scale. There are a few things that can be done to reduce the memory footprint, such as using a 64-bit JVM, using a compressed heap, and using a low-memory profile.

Finally, it is also important to focus on the application's runtime performance. There are a few things that can be done to improve runtime performance, such as using a caching solution, using a connection pool, and using a message queue.

Design patterns and architectural considerations for Spring Boot applications.

Spring Boot is designed to simplify the bootstrapping and development of a new Spring application. It provides a wide range of features that can be used to develop, test, deploy and monitor Spring-based applications.

When designing a Spring Boot application, there are a number of design patterns and architectural considerations that should be taken into account.

The first consideration is the use of the Model-View-Controller (MVC) pattern. Spring Boot applications are typically designed using this pattern, which separates the application into three distinct layers: the model, the view, and the controller.

The model layer is responsible for managing the data and business logic of the application. The view layer is responsible for generating the user interface. The controller layer is responsible for handling user requests and invoking the appropriate actions in the model and view layers.

Another important consideration is the use of dependency injection. Spring Boot applications are typically designed with dependency injection in mind. This means that dependencies between different parts of the application are injected into the application at runtime, rather than being hard-coded into the application.

This has a number of benefits, including the ability to more easily change the implementation of a dependency, and the ability to more easily unit test the application.

Finally, it is important to consider the use of Spring Security when designing a Spring Boot application. Spring Security is a framework that provides a number of features that can be used to secure a Spring-based application.

Some of the features that can be used with Spring Security include authentication, authorization, and access control.

When designing a Spring Boot application, it is important to consider all of these factors in order to create a well-designed and secure application.

Utilizing Spring Boot's support for messaging and event-driven architectures.

Spring Boot provides great support for messaging and event-driven architectures. It makes it easy to send and receive messages from a variety of sources, including JMS, AMQP, and STOMP. It also provides support for message converters, error handling, and message-driven POJOs.

Exploring advanced topics, such as Spring Batch for batch processing or Spring WebFlux for reactive programming.

Spring Batch is a framework for batch processing that allows developers to write concise and maintainable code. It is a lightweight solution that can be easily integrated with other frameworks and libraries. Spring Batch provides support for both traditional and modern batch processing scenarios.

Spring WebFlux is a reactive programming framework for building web applications. It is a non-blocking alternative to the traditional blocking Java web frameworks. Spring WebFlux allows developers to write concise and maintainable code. It is a lightweight solution that can be easily integrated with other frameworks and libraries.

www.ingramcontent.com/pod-product-compliance
Lightning Source LLC
LaVergne TN
LVHW051706050326
832903LV00032B/4039